RHINOCEROS

VS.

TRICERATOPS

BY CHARLES C. HOFER

CAPSTONE PRESS
a capstone imprint

Published by Capstone Press, an imprint of Capstone.
1710 Roe Crest Drive, North Mankato, Minnesota 56003
capstonepub.com

Library of Congress Cataloging-in-Publication Data
Names: Hofer, Charles, author.
Title: Rhinoceros vs. triceratops / by Charles C. Hofer.
Description: North Mankato, Minnesota : Capstone Press, [2024] | Series:
    Beastly battles | Includes bibliographical references and index. | Audience: Ages 9-11
    Audience: Grades 4-6
Summary: "It's a clash between two horned beasts! The rhinoceros is one of the largest animals living on land today. But millions of years ago, the triceratops was one of the biggest and most powerful beasts of its time. Learn what makes these similar creatures so impressive. Then decide which tanklike beast would achieve victory in a fight"—Provided by publisher.
Identifiers: LCCN 2023019001 (print) | LCCN 2023019002 (ebook) | ISBN 9781669065128 (hardcover) | ISBN 9781669065302 (paperback) | ISBN 9781669065166 (pdf) | ISBN 9781669065326 (kindle edition) | ISBN 9781669065319 (epub)
Subjects: LCSH: Rhinoceroses—Juvenile literature. | Triceratops—Juvenile literature.
    Classification: LCC QL737.U63 H54 2024 (print) | LCC QL737.U63 (ebook)
    DDC 599.66/8—dc23/eng/20230627
LC record available at https://lccn.loc.gov/2023019001
LC ebook record available at https://lccn.loc.gov/2023019002

Editorial Credits
Editor: Aaron Sautter; Designer: Bobbie Nuytten; Media Researcher:
Rebekah Hubstenberger: Production Specialist: Whitney Schaefer

Image Credits
Alamy: Science Photo Library, 5 (bottom), Steve Bloom Images, 14; Capstone: Jon Hughes, 13 (triceratops); Getty Images: Freder, 20, iStock/Emma Sanger-Horwell, 10, iStock/foto76, 25, iStock/GlobalP, 28, iStock/PaulGregg, 11, iStock/Utopia_88, 15, iStock/Warpaintcobra, 27, iStock/wrangel, 24, Karl Ammann, 21, Manoj Shah, 26; Science Source: Jose Antonio Penas, 22, QA International, 29; Shutterstock: David Roland, 23, DM7, 19, Dotted Yeti, Cover (bottom), FOTOGRIN, 7, Herschel Hoffmeyer, Cover (bottom background), 9, 13 (background), 17, Papa Bravo, Cover (top), VladisloveM, 5 (top)

All internet sites appearing in back matter were available and accurate when this book was sent to press.

TABLE OF CONTENTS

Words in **bold** are in the glossary.

A CLASH OF HORNS!

It's a battle of powerful, horned beasts! Both are strong and tough. They're built for battle.

One is an **ancient** creature from long ago. The other is one of today's strongest living animals.

Who would win this clash between huge, horned beasts?

RHINOCEROS

TRICERATOPS

MEET THE WHITE RHINOCEROS

There are five **species** of rhinoceros living around the world. The white rhino is the largest. It grows two horns on its **snout**.

The white rhino is big and strong. It lives in Africa. White rhinos like to live in open, grassy areas.

THREE-HORNED BEAST

Triceratops was a giant dinosaur. It lived about 66 million years ago. Triceratops lived in western North America.

Triceratops means "three-horned face." It had three huge horns on its head and snout. The longer horns grew up to 3 feet (1 meter) long.

BIG AND BAD

The white rhino is the world's second largest land animal. Only elephants grow bigger.

White rhinos can grow to about 12 feet (3.7 m) long. They can weigh more than 7,000 pounds (3,175 kilograms). That's as big as a pickup truck! Few animals will mess with a white rhino.

DANGEROUS DINOSAUR

Triceratops was grew up to 30 feet (9 m) long. It weighed as much as 16,000 pounds (7,260 kg). That's bigger than an African elephant! Only the biggest and baddest dinos would mess with Triceratops.

CHARGE!

The white rhino can run fast over a short distance. It can reach about 30 miles (44 kilometers) per hour.

White rhinos live near **predators** like lions. When threatened, a rhino might **charge**. This action will scare off a hungry lion.

STANDING STRONG

Triceratops had short legs. It was pretty slow. It could not outrun predators. Instead, it stood strong against enemies. These big dinos often fought hungry predators like Tyrannosaurus rex.

BONE BREAKER

Triceratops had a hard **beak**, like a bird. It helped the dino strip leaves from plants. The beak was strong enough to crack open coconuts. Triceratops may have used its beak to break an enemy's bones.

STAY SHARP!

A white rhino's horn can grow to about 40 inches (102 centimeters) long. Rhinos use their sharp horns to defend themselves and their young.

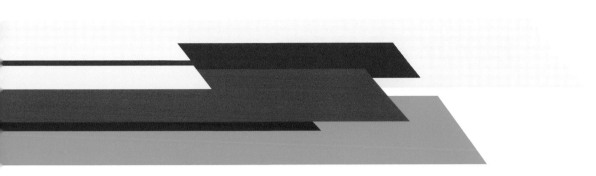

White rhinos can be very **aggressive**.
They will charge at anything. They will
even charge toward a larger elephant!

BODY ARMOR

Triceratops is famous for its **frill**. It was like a bony shell that covered the dino's neck. It likely helped protect Triceratops from predators. It may have also helped the dinosaur stay cool.

FRILL

TOUGH,
SCALY SKIN

Triceratops's skin was like armor. It was covered in scales. It's armor-covered skin helped protect the beast from hungry dinosaurs.

THICK SKIN

White rhinos have tough skin too. Their skin can be up to 2 inches (5 cm) thick. That's more than 10 times thicker than human skin!

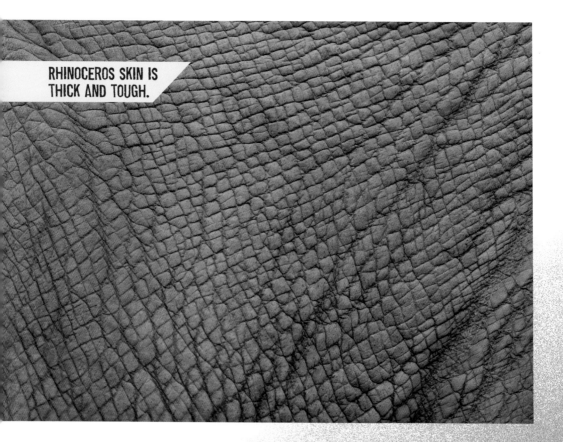

RHINOCEROS SKIN IS THICK AND TOUGH.

Rhinos need their tough, armor-like skin.

They have poor **eyesight**. Their tough skin

helps protect them from predator attacks.

BEASTLY BRAWL!

It's time for a beastly battle! A big white rhino faces off against Triceratops. The beast stomps at the ground. Will it charge?

But Triceratops seems unafraid. It stands its ground to keep an eye on the rhino.

What will happen next in this showdown of horned beasts?

WHO'S THE WINNER?

Triceratops is huge and powerful. But the white rhino is strong and aggressive. Both have big, sharp horns. Which of these armored foes will win?

	White Rhinoceros	**Triceratops**
HABITAT	grasslands in Africa	western North America
WEIGHT	7,000 pounds (3,175 kg)	16,000 pounds (7,260 kg)
LENGTH	12 feet (3.7 meters)	30 feet (9 m)
TOP SPEED	30 mph (44 kph)	unknown
WEAPONS	two big, strong horns up to 40 inches (102 cm) long	three huge, sharp horns up to 3 feet (1 m) long
DEFENSES	thick, tough skin	• sharp, horned beak • tough, scaly skin • protective frill
STRATEGY	aggressive, charges to attack	stood its ground, used frill and horns for defense

GLOSSARY

aggressive (uh-GREH-siv)—ready to attack

ancient (AYN-shunt)—from a long time ago

beak (BEEK)—the hard front part of the mouth of birds and some dinosaurs

charge (CHARJ)—to rush at in order to attack

eyesight (AHY-sahyt)—the ability to see

frill (FRIL)—a bony collar that fans out around an animal's neck

predator (PRED-uh-tur)—an animal that hunts other animals for food

snout (SNOUT)—the long, front part of an animal's head, including the nose, mouth, and jaws

species (SPEE-sheez)—a group of animals with similar features

READ MORE

Anderson, Josh. *Horned Dinos*. Parker, CO:
The Child's World, 2023.

Markovics, Joyce L. *Northern White Rhino*.
Ann Arbor, MI: Cherry Lake Publishing, 2023.

Radley, Gail. *Triceratops*. Mankato, MN:
Black Rabbit Books, 2021.

INTERNET SITES

Active Wild: Triceratops Facts
activewild.com/triceratops-facts-for-kids-
students-adults/

DK Findout!: Triceratops
dkfindout.com/us/dinosaurs-and-prehistoric-life/
dinosaurs/triceratops/

DK Findout!: White Rhinoceros
dkfindout.com/us/animals-and-nature/
rhinoceroses/white-rhinoceros/

INDEX

ABOUT THE AUTHOR

Charles C. Hofer is a writer and biologist living in the western United States, not far from where Triceratops once roamed across the land.